101
CORPORATE
HAIKU

Characters (*kanji*) on the title page and at the beginning of each section were executed in traditional brush strokes by master calligrapher Gundi Chan.

101
CORPORATE
HAIKU

WILLIAM WARRINER

♦ **Addison-Wesley Publishing Company**
Reading, Massachusetts   Menlo Park, California   New York
Don Mills, Ontario   Wokingham, England   Amsterdam   Bonn
Sydney   Singapore   Tokyo   Madrid   San Juan
Paris   Seoul   Milan   Mexico City   Taipei

To David and Dawn

Library of Congress Cataloging-in-Publication Data

Warriner, William
    101 corporate haiku / William Warriner.
        p.   cm.
    ISBN 0-201-40942-9
    1. Business—Poetry. 2. Haiku, American. I. Title. II. Title:
One hundred one corporate haiku. III. Title: One hundred and one
corporate haiku.
PS3573.A7798A615   1994
811'.54—dc20   94-18234
                                                                CIP

Cover design by Suzanne Heiser
Text design by Karen Battles
Set in 16-point Garamond 3 by Battles Design

1 2 3 4 5 6 7 8 9 - BAA- 9897969594
First printing, October 1994

Addison-Wesley books are available at special discounts for bulk purchases. For more information, please contact:
Corporate, Government, and Special Sales Department
Addison-Wesley Publishing Company
Reading, MA 01867
(800) 238-9682

CONTENTS

MEMORANDUM

TO: All Concerned
FROM: W.W.
SUBJECT: Corporate Haiku

Sixty million Americans spend a third of their lives working for corporations, but nobody writes songs about that. Instead, we write manuals: how to compete, implement, re-engineer, upgrade, down-size, rightsize, optimize, and offload. We have killed poetry, and most of us were too busy meeting deadlines to attend the funeral.

But poetry is alive and well in Japan, in the form of haiku. Having already learned about "total quality," theory Z, and *kaizen* from Japan, maybe we can take another lesson.

After all, corporate enterprise is hurting for metaphors. Look how much time we spend paradigm-hunting. We end up with a short shortlist: the art of war and the teamwork of sports. Very brave, but is that all there is? What about learning from the structure of a tree, the strategy of a spider, or the flight plan of a flock of ducks? Haiku can open windows of perception.

The Japanese haiku dates back to the time of the *Mayflower* voyage and has even older roots in China. Plenty of time to de-velop an elaborate rulebook. In America, they teach us only one rule for haiku: three lines, distributed into five, seven, and five syllables. Seventeen syllables is no arbitrary number. It equals one healthy lungful of air. When you capture a thought in one breath, you quickly drop those fat buzzwords you used in your memo on organizational restructuring. Haiku are rightsized for us: a dozen will fit inside a coffee break.

Traditional haiku collections are arranged by seasons of the year. A proper haiku is glued to its season like we are glued to this fiscal quarter. It includes "season-words" called *kigo*, to hint at where we are on the calendar.

Serious American poets have treated haiku with great reverence. But a long face is not mandatory. The term was built from two Chinese characters that mean "playful phrases." Some haiku are simply riddles—a two-line question plus a one-line answer. And there's a long tradition of haiku as satire, called *senryu*.

In poetry as in management theory, rules are for breaking. Even the classical poets messed around with the five-seven-five formula. The nineteenth-century Japanese poet Shiki okayed a range of haiku from fifteen to twenty-five syllables.

But there is one rule with no exceptions. Dr. Kenneth Yasuda, in his book *The Japanese Haiku*, said, "All haiku worthy of the name are records of...an instant of insight." Which means, the last line of any decent haiku is always a surprise. A twist. A punch line, if you will.

The haiku in this book break a few rules, including those of corporate decorum. They are unauthorized and a tad subversive; I hope they may inspire you to some unauthorized writing of your own.

FIRST QUARTER

1

Snowdrifts rule the world;
civilization is lost
inside my briefcase.

2

Somewhere in Japan,
they will design a car that
plows its own driveway.

<u>3</u>

Before first light, while
I dream of deadlines, rises
the Entrepreneur.

4

Rabbit and dog tracks
cross the snow: tell me timing
isn't everything.

<u>5</u>

Hopelessly entranced
by the flight of numbers, I
no longer see birds.

6

Danger lurks, where a
crushing avalanche of white
has buried my desk.

<u>7</u>

Objects reflected
in a project schedule are
closer than they seem.

8

This is my space: I
am content, where ivy grows
on a computer.

<u>9</u>

We have come into
a world of mystery, and
words like *WYSIWYG*.

10

Slowly, we acquire
management proficiency
in slipping schedules.

_11_

The clocks disagree;
yet they all accuse me of
mismanaging time.

12

Solemn white gowns haunt
the lab: we are possessed by
a phantom product.

_13_

By the vanishing
quantities of Quality,
I am now pursued.

14

My task is to go
where no one has gone before—
and invent the wheel.

15

Pale in the moonlight,
a blank page waits, beckoning,
a moving target.

16

Savor a deadline;
it is merely an excuse
to stay up all night.

_17_

Time zones are magic:
calling the East that lies West,
I call tomorrow.

_18_

But how can this be?
My Teacher commands me: Press
ENTER to exit.

<u>*19*</u>

Two sides of one wall:
over there sits yesterday.
Here sits tomorrow.

20

In the glass towers
of this town, old ideas
are cast in concrete.

_21_

Twice the light comes to
a corner office; I wait
for twice the vision.

22

The ponderous ice
of glaciers flows faster than
my corporation.

<u>23</u>

The Strategist is
adept in the ancient art
of expense accounts.

24

A tropical beach,
at last. I trace in the sand
a lazy spreadsheet.

25

My glass is half full—
and the waiter brings
an empty fortune cookie.

SECOND QUARTER

_26_

The snow is gone; trees
swell with sap. In no way can
my proposal fail.

27

An ambitious kite
flies free—it seems to say,
This Space Available.

_28_

A mushroom has pushed
through stone; it knows the art of
negotiation.

<u>29</u>

Outside my window,
just one week each year, lilacs
are the bottom line.

<u>30</u>

A marketing bird!
He tells me, tells me, and then
tells what he told me.

31

The first MBA
of spring has perched, supported
by an ancient branch.

32

He has a certain
sense that history begins
with his arrival.

_33_

I know by that stare
he can reach no decision—
taxidermy eyes.

_34_

Nothing there but fog...
and no light can penetrate
that memorandum.

_35_

A duel at dawn:
and the chosen weapon is
a power breakfast.

36

As a general
studies the whole battlefield,
learn your enemy.

_37_

One nagging instinct
pursues and stings him: never
be accountable.

38

Thorns block my pathway
to the sunlight—ten thousand
little managers.

<u>39</u>

Above the nest of
R & D, slowly circle
marketing vultures.

_40_

Enlightened beaver,
he has built a lodge without
corner offices.

_41_

So many birdsongs.
In this conference, each sings
its own agenda.

42

The road we follow
leads to Mount Fuji, if we
get past this meeting.

_43_

By some mystery
of scent, we know our places
around the table.

_44_

At the projector,
a spider traces a map
of his marketplace.

<u>45</u>

With care, the spider
navigates its web—so with
my strategic plan.

46

Pouring rain outside;
in our meeting, it's raining
apples and oranges.

<u>47</u>

Our marketing plan:
Though it be a small one,
sell it as a large one.

_48_

Hark! I hear a beep!
Somewhere a newborn machine
cries for attention.

_49_

An unmoved seagull
faces the wind, holding down
its installed base.

_50_

It's two A.M., and
I am watching CNN;
I must get a life.

THIRD QUARTER

_51_

Heat shimmers from cars
surrounding my parking space;
they all want my job.

52

Safe in his garden,
the caretaker tends his turf,
a true CEO.

_53_

Seeking paradigms,
I find it always helps to
see people as ants.

<u>54</u>

Ants toiling in line
bear fragments of leaves; each cuts
its own parachute.

55

Ants understand: they
climb both over and under
a chain of command.

56

A hundred horns sound
fanfares for the Emperor's
newest product launch.

57

The ballrooms of old
glitter only with the light
of graphs and pie charts.

_58_

A podium calls
for words of Power, turning
truth to ritual.

_59_

Hear the numbers sing!
Through a forest of words come
glimpses of the truth.

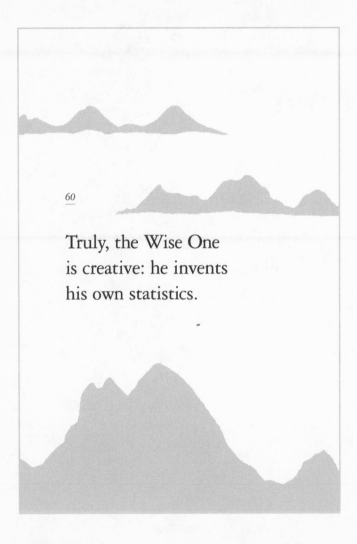

_60_

Truly, the Wise One
is creative: he invents
his own statistics.

61

A celebration!
In a grand hotel, a feast
of Lucite trophies.

62

Out at the ballpark,
my CEO studies his
management theory.

63

Gray hairs! This must be
the right moment to assert
my vintage wisdom.

64

Fields of white daisies
gently nod consensus as
I rehearse my speech.

65

Remember to thank
the little people—for the
years they slowed you down.

66

Heavy silence fills
the room and points to me—I
spoke the truth too soon.

67

I walk past miles of
walls built stone by stone, learning
to respect old work.

_68_

Two eyes in the grass:
nothing there to fear—just a
sneaking suspicion.

<u>69</u>

Lone bee in the field,
only you know the source of
beehive salaries.

_70_

So beautiful, the
poison ivy, as it chokes
a weeping willow.

<u>71</u>

A twig snaps; the woods
are alert. A beginning—
or maybe an end.

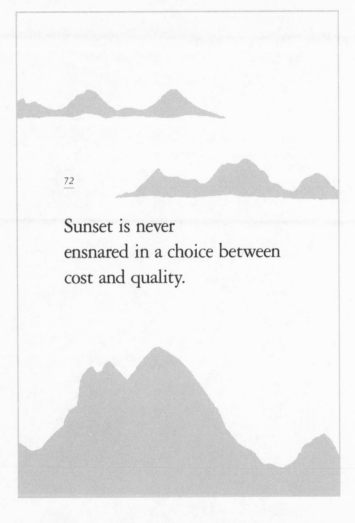

_72_

Sunset is never
ensnared in a choice between
cost and quality.

73

A buzz, then silence.
He, for one, can be trusted:
the fly in my soup.

_74_

No moon and no rhyme,
no reason, no blossoms, I
drink my Chardonnay.

_75_

In adversity,
just what does the Wise One do?
And where is Square One?

FOURTH QUARTER

76

In Big Sky country
I roam, testing freedom and
my Gold Card limit.

77

It takes a great heart
to view the Rockies as a
sales territory.

78

Geese honking southward—
do their cries say they follow
the Way of the Dow?

79

Fire in the river:
salmon drive upstream. O, why
did I hire guppies?

_80_

An old woodcarver,
his decisions on the floor,
builds by downsizing.

81

A flight of birds splits
into factions, arguing
about migration.

82

Light dawns with a thud.
All those apples on the ground—
which one was Newton's?

83

My cat on a hot
car hood, gathering warmth—is
this why I commute?

84

At my desk I read
executive summaries,
so to rule the world.

85

The Wise One teaches
without words; I follow his
Unwritten Rulebook.

86

Thus it is unwritten:
never shall be heard
a negative word.

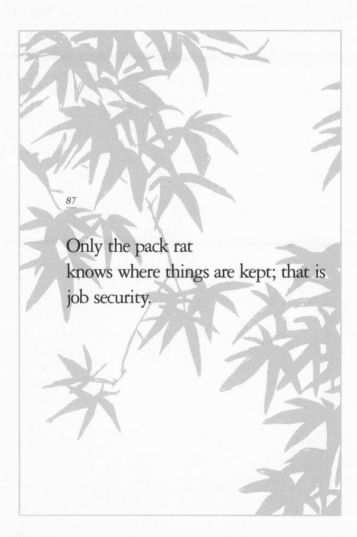

87

Only the pack rat
knows where things are kept; that is
job security.

88

A safe prediction
for the market is the time
of the closing bell.

89

As cherry blossoms
fall, so fall the dynasties
of a free market.

90

The Wise One is most
subtle. I think his thoughts, and
think they are my own.

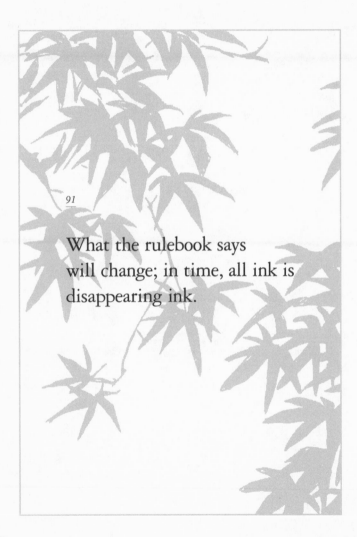

91

What the rulebook says
will change; in time, all ink is
disappearing ink.

_92_

This old building stands
above our quarrels inside,
watching its trees grow.

93

Hushed voices echo
in the halls. From the boardroom,
sounds like locking horns.

94

What makes a samurai
step down from his high horse?
A few bad quarters.

95

In youth, we learned that
a company must grow; now
we teach it to shrink.

96

Is it the greatest
glory of a leaf, when it
flies free from the tree?

97

In those packing crates
hides a bold new vision of
my next enterprise.

_98_

Last year's proposal.
Add wings; then it will become
a new idea.

99

Under a blue sky
I can become a
virtual corporation.

100

A long winding road
becomes the shortest distance
between two ideas.

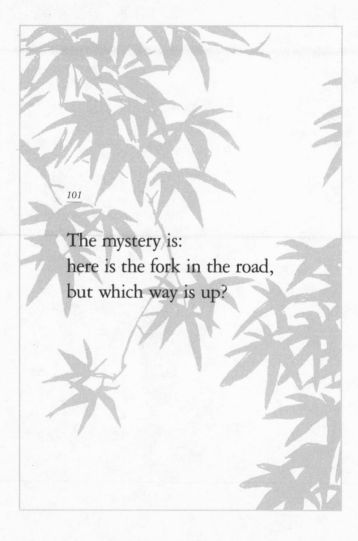

101

The mystery is:
here is the fork in the road,
but which way is up?